TAKE THE LEAD

TRUMPET

BIG HITS

Editorial, production and recording: Artemis Music Limited • Design and production: Space DPS Limited • Published 2004

RESPECT
THE VALUE OF
MUSIC

IMP

International MUSIC Publications

5 Colours In Her Hair

Demonstration   Backing

Words and Music by James Bourne,
Tom Fletcher and Daniel Jones

Driving rock tempo

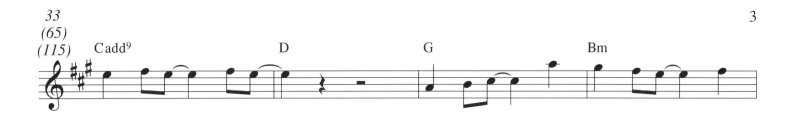

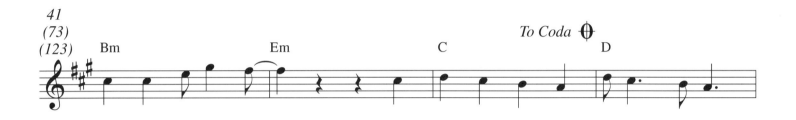

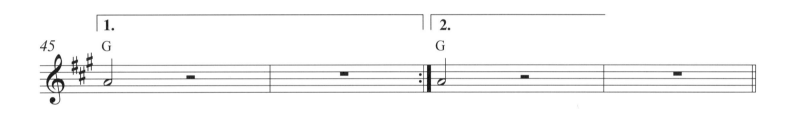

Air Hostess

Demonstration   Backing

Words and Music by James Bourne,
Tom Fletcher, Mathew Sargeant and Charlie Simpson

Driving pop tempo

⊕ CODA

Amazing

Demonstration Backing

Words and Music by
Jonathan Douglas and George Michael

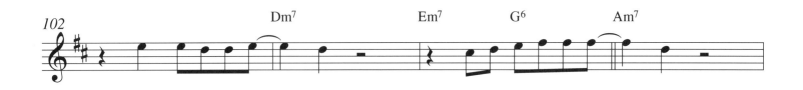

The Show

Words and Music by Miranda Cooper,
Brian Higgins, Timothy Powell,
Lisa Cowling and Jonathan Shave

© 2004 Xenomania Music Ltd
Warner/Chappell Music Publishing Ltd, London W6 8BS

12

Changes

Demonstration   Backing

Words and Music by Terence Butler,
John Osbourne, William Ward and Tony Iommi

Mysterious Girl

Demonstration

Backing

Words and Music by Oliver Jacobs,
Phillip Jacobs, Glen Goldsmith,
Peter Andre and Anthony Wayne

Medium reggae tempo

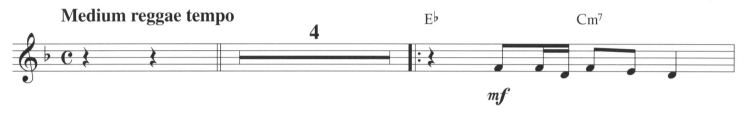

Sunrise

Words and Music by
Norah Jones and Lee Alexander

EMI Music Publishing Ltd, London WC2H 0QY

Single

Demonstration   Backing

Words and Music by
Andrew Frampton, Natasha Bedingfield,
Stephen Kipner and Wayne Wilkins

Steady pop tempo

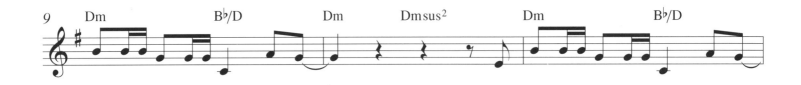

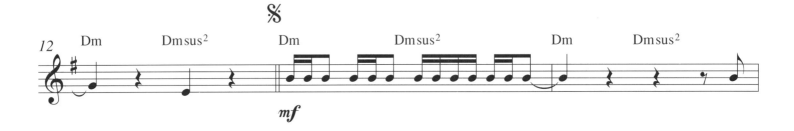

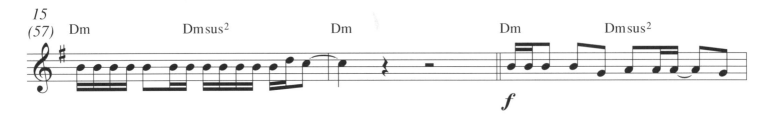

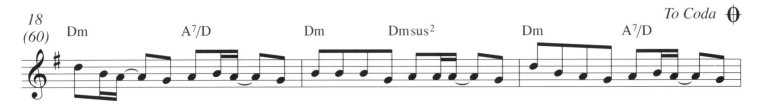

YOU'RE THE VOICE

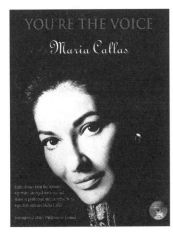

8861A PV/CD
Casta Diva from Norma – Vissi D'arte from Tosca – Un Bel Di Vedremo from Madama Butterfly – Addio, Del Passato from La Traviata – J'ai Perdu Mon Eurydice from Orphee Et Eurydice – Les Tringles Des Sistres Tintaient from Carmen – Porgi Amor from Le Nozze Di Figaro – Ave Maria from Otello

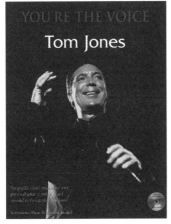

8860A PVG/CD
Delilah – Green Green Grass Of Home – Help Yourself – I'll Never Fall In Love Again – It's Not Unusual – Mama Told Me Not To Come – Sexbomb – Thunderball – What's New Pussycat – You Can Leave Your Hat On

9297A PVG/CD
Beauty And The Beast – Because You Loved Me – Falling Into You – The First Time Ever I Saw Your Face – It's All Coming Back To Me Now – Misled – My Heart Will Go On – The Power Of Love – Think Twice – When I Fall In Love

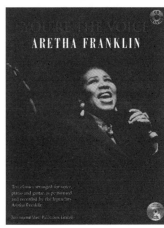

9349A PVG/CD
Chain Of Fools – A Deeper Love Do Right Woman, Do Right Man – I Knew You Were Waiting (For Me) – I Never Loved A Man (The Way I Loved You) – I Say A Little Prayer – Respect – Think – Who's Zooming Who – (You Make Me Feel Like) A Natural Woman

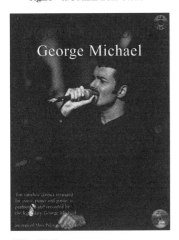

9007A PVG/CD
Careless Whisper – A Different Corner – Faith – Father Figure – Freedom '90 – I'm Your Man – I Knew You Were Waiting (For Me) – Jesus To A Child – Older – Outside

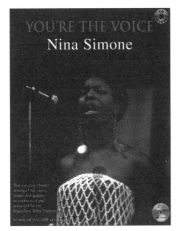

9606A PVG/CD
Don't Let Me Be Misunderstood – Feeling Good – I Loves You Porgy – I Put A Spell On You – Love Me Or Leave Me – Mood Indigo – My Baby Just Cares For Me – Ne Me Quitte Pas (If You Go Away) – Nobody Knows You When You're Down And Out – Take Me To The Water

9700A PVG/CD
Beautiful – Crying In The Rain – I Feel The Earth Move – It's Too Late – (You Make Me Feel Like) A Natural Woman – So Far Away – Way Over Yonder – Where You Lead – Will You Love Me Tomorrow – You've Got A Friend

9746A PVG/CD
April In Paris – Come Rain Or Come Shine – Fly Me To The Moon (In Other Words) – I've Got You Under My Skin – The Lady Is A Tramp – My Kinda Town (Chicago Is) – My Way – Theme From *New York, New York* – Someone To Watch Over Me – Something Stupid

9770A PVG/CD
Cry Me A River – Evergreen (A Star Is Born) – Happy Days Are Here Again – I've Dreamed Of You – Memory – My Heart Belongs To Me – On A Clear Day (You Can See Forever) – Someday My Prince Will Come – Tell Him (duet with Celine Dion) – The Way We Were

9799A PVG/CD
Boogie Woogie Bugle Boy – Chapel Of Love – Friends – From A Distance – Hello In There – One For My Baby (And One More For The Road) – Only In Miami – The Rose – When A Man Loves A Woman – Wind Beneath My Wings

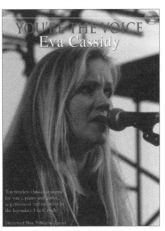

9810A PVG/CD
Ain't No Sunshine – Autumn Leaves – How Can I Keep From Singing – Imagine – It Doesn't Matter Anymore – Over The Rainbow – Penny To My Name – People Get Ready – Wayfaring Stranger – What A Wonderful World

9889A PVG/CD
Around The World – Born Free – From Russia With Love – Gonna Build A Mountain – The Impossible Dream – My Kind Of Girl – On A Clear Day You Can See Forever – Portrait Of My Love – Softly As I Leave You – Walk Away

The outstanding vocal series from IMP

CD contains full backings for each song, professionally arranged to recreate the sounds of the original recording

Essential Audition Songs

Broadway (Female)
7171A   Book and CD

Broadway (Male)
9185A   Book and CD

Pop Ballads (Female)
6939A   Book and CD

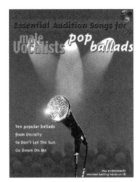

Pop Ballads (Male)
9776A   Book and CD

Pop Divas
7769A   Book and CD

Kids
7341A   Book and CD

Jazz Standards
7021A   Book and CD

Timeless Crooners
9495A   Book and CD

Duets
7432A   Book and CD

Movie Hits
9186A   Book and CD

Wannabe Pop Stars
9735A   Book and CD

Love Songs
9841A   Book and CD

Big Band Hits
9725A   Book and CD

West End Hits
10009A   Book and CD